SOMETIMES I DON'T LIKE TO TALK
(BUT SOMETIMES I CAN'T KEEP QUIET!)

By Jessica Lamb-Shapiro

Plainview, New York

**Sometimes I Don't Like to Talk
(But Sometimes I Can't Keep Quiet!)**

by Jessica Lamb-Shapiro
Illustrated by Robin C. Morris

Childswork/Childsplay publishes products for mental health professionals, teachers, and parents who wish to help children with their developmental, social, and emotional growth. For questions, comments, or to request a free catalog describing hundreds of games, toys, books, and other counseling tools, call
1-800-962-1141.

No part of this book may be reproduced or transmitted in any form or by any means, electronic or mechanical, including photocopying, recording, or by any information storage and retrieval system without written permission from the publisher.

© 2002 Childswork/Childsplay, LLC
A Guidance Channel Company
135 Dupont Street
Plainview, NY 11803

All rights reserved.
Printed in the United States of America

ISBN 1-58815-045-3

Introduction for Adults

The main characteristic of shyness is extreme concern about social evaluation by others, and in particular, oversensitivity to rejection. Shy children are so concerned about being rejected that they will do almost anything to avoid calling attention to themselves. They will keep to themselves and avoid taking risks or trying new things. Sometimes, like Emmy, the main character in this story, they will hardly even talk.

Shyness is a much more common and serious problem than many people realize. In fact, the fear of being rejected by others is among the most common human fears. In a survey of three thousand people, nearly 42 percent of the respondents said they considered themselves shy, and nearly 80 percent said they had been shy at some point in their lives. The majority of those who labeled themselves as shy described this trait as a serious problem that interfered with their lives.

Shyness in children can have both short- and long-term adverse effects:

- Shy children typically underachieve in school.
- Shy children have a lowered sense of self-worth that places them at greater risk for depression.
- Shy children tend to have more physical health problems, because they don't tell people about their early symptoms.
- Shy children have fewer social experiences and more difficulty making friends as adolescents and adults.

While almost all children experience shyness sometimes, it is important to identify children who suffer because of their shyness. Researchers tell us there are two basic types of shy children. Shy introverts are obvious to us, because they do not try to hide their fear of social criticism. Shy extroverts are actually very outgoing, but behind their smiles and laughter, they worry about every social encounter.

Shyness is not a problem that ever goes away completely, but the earlier children receive help for their shyness, the more like they are to be able to cope with this problem and keep it from affecting other aspects of their development.

It is our hope that this book will help shy children see that they are not alone with their problem and that adults can help them overcome it. As in Emmy's story, supportive adults must help shy children slowly learn that their worst fears of rejection will not be realized. Each new experience of speaking in class or taking a social risk will help them learn that sometimes it is fine to be quiet, but sometimes it's more fun to make all the noise that you want.

Lawrence E. Shapiro, Ph.D.
Series Editor

I used to be pretty quiet. In fact, I used to hardly talk at all! I talked at home when I had something to say.

But I'd never talk at school.

My name is Emmy. I'm pretty shy and that's why I didn't like to talk.

People used to call me "Emmy the Mouse" at school, because I was as quiet as a mouse.

But I'm not so shy and quiet anymore. Sometimes, I like to scare my little brother.

BOO!

Or I make monster faces.

ARRRRRRGH!

Now, I'll tell you the story of how I stopped being so shy and quiet. If you're shy and quiet too, it could even help you.

I have always been scared about going to school. All the kids were always friendly with each other, and I didn't know if they'd like me. In class, I was afraid of giving the wrong answer to the teacher's questions. What if everyone laughed at me?

I decided I'd better say just nothing at all.

Sometimes, I'd have nightmares about school. There was one I used to have all the time. In my dream, I'd be called on by the teacher. But when I opened my mouth, a squeak came out.

Then I turned into a mouse! This made everyone laugh, and I ran away into a little mouse hole.

Sometimes I wished there was a real mouse hole at school that I could hide in.

My parents had a hard time understanding why I was so quiet. They knew there was nothing wrong with my voice. I could talk fine at home, just quietly. People can't help it if they are quiet. Can they? But sometimes my parents got mad at me for being too quiet.

One time we went to a big family picnic. All the other kids were playing and laughing and running around. I brought a book and just read it by myself. When we got home, my dad said, "Why are you so quiet all the time? People are going to think there is something wrong with you if you are always so quiet."

My dad's face turned red, and he looked angry. I don't think it's right to be mad at someone, just because they're quiet. Do you?

When Dad gets mad, I feel like being even quieter.

Sometimes, my teacher would get mad at me too.

I remember one time my teacher asked, "Emmy, who is the President of the United States?" I knew the answer, but I didn't want to say it. Instead, I just looked at the floor. "What's the answer?" she asked me again. But I didn't want to talk. "Emmy, I know you know the answer." I wouldn't look at her, but I could hear from her voice that she was mad at me. "Okay, Emmy," she said. "If you don't want to talk, then don't talk."

That night, my teacher called my parents to tell them I was having a problem at school. I thought I was in real trouble!

The next day when we were eating breakfast, my mother told me I was going to see the school counselor.

"Why?" I asked my mother. "Am I in trouble?" "No, not at all," Mom said. "The school counselor is just going to talk to you about being shy."

The school counselor's name was Mrs. Anthony.

She didn't have a classroom like my teacher's. She had an office. She had lots of books in her office, and pictures on the wall that looked like kids had drawn them. She even had toys and games in her office, which made me feel like seeing her might not be too bad.

I liked seeing Mrs. Anthony because she didn't try to make me talk. She let me play with the toys and draw pictures. It was pretty cool, and it was better than being in class where people can make fun of you or get mad at you.

Mrs. Anthony said she knew many children who were shy like me and didn't like to talk. She said sometimes people don't realize they make things worse for shy children when they try to make them talk, or get mad at them for not talking.

Mrs. Anthony said, "I am going to talk to your parents and your teacher. I'll help them find ways to make it easier for you to talk more. That way, people can get to know you better and see what a smart and interesting girl you are."

Mrs. Anthony told my parents and teacher about other ways for me to communicate in class.

She said many shy children find it easier to draw pictures, or write notes, or even use the computer to send messages. I wasn't sure if I liked this or not. I don't like to be different from other kids. But it was better than having to talk.

My teacher said it would be a good idea if we spent a few minutes talking together every day…just her and me.

Sometimes we could talk before school, and other times at recess. Sometimes I could stay after school if I wanted to. She said it would be my choice.

A few weeks later, my counselor came into my classroom and talked to my teacher and me. They both thought I was ready to talk more in class, but I should do it just a little bit at a time.

Mrs. Anthony said, "This week your teacher will ask you to spell one word during your spelling period. She will call on you first, so you won't have to wait and worry about it. You're a good speller, so you will probably get it right. But even if you make a mistake, that's okay. Soon you will see that everyone makes mistakes sometimes… even your parents, and your teacher, and me."

My teacher also changed the groups in our class. She put me in a group with other children who were quiet too. (Before I had been in a group with Billy and Kylie, who were very loud and always making trouble.)

Soon I felt comfortable working in my group. Sometimes we'd hang out together at recess. We liked to talk together.

Then one day, Kylie talked to me after class. She said, "Emmy, I know you are quiet, but I don't think you are as quiet as a mouse. I'm not going to call you Emmy the Mouse anymore."

That made me feel so good. I said, "Thank you." Kylie said, "You're welcome."

My dad read me a story about a mouse who was really quiet. One day, the mouse saw a big, mean cat sneaking up on her little brother mouse. She needed to save him! She called to him in her little mouse voice, but he didn't hear. The mouse was really scared. She tried again, but he still didn't hear.

The other mice saw her problem and came to help. Together, they called to him in bigger and bigger and bigger voices, until the little brother mouse heard and ran away to safety!

That was a good story. It made me think of how all the people helping me—my parents, teachers, and friends—were like all those mice. Together, they helped me.

Now I'm still not the biggest talker in class, but I'm not the quietest either. And when I do talk, no one laughs.

Now, Kylie is my best friend and I like to talk with her all the time. Sometimes she says, "Take a break, Emmy. You're talking too much!"

Talking is a good thing for kids to do. Besides, if I couldn't talk, I couldn't tell you this story!

The End